SCHOLASTIC

FUN FLAPS
1ST 100 SIGHT WORDS

Violet Findley

New York • Toronto • London
Auckland • Sydney • New Delhi • Hong Kong

Cover and interior design: Michelle H. Kim
Cover photo: Adam Chinitz
Illustrations: The Noun Project

Scholastic Inc., 557 Broadway, New York, NY 10012
ISBN: 978-1-338-60313-2
Copyright © 2020 by Scholastic Inc.
Published by Scholastic Inc. All rights reserved.
Printed in the U.S.A.
First printing, January 2020.

2 3 4 5 6 7 8 9 10   40   25 24 23 22 21

Table of Contents

INTRODUCTION

Dear Educator,

Welcome to *Fun Flaps: 1st 100 Sight Words*! These hands-on manipulatives will make learning the first 100 sight words from the Fry List easy and irresistible.

What are sight words? Sight words are those bland connective words—*the, of, a, and, with, you, for, it*—that are essential to text, but often a challenge to define and decode. In fact, research shows that as much as 70 percent of everything we read is comprised of them. Predictably, research *also* shows that children with the ability to automatically recognize sight words are on course to become confident, successful readers. But how do busy teachers and their students find the time?

Enter Fun Flaps! These playful, kinesthetic learning tools will help kids master this important list of words once and for all. Fun Flaps are a great way to foster classroom friendships *and* enrich family time—just reproduce, fold, and they're ready to use with partners or caregivers. Also, because children are challenged to read sentences aloud, they boost oral language facility. And here's more good news: The book is stocked with companion practice pages to provide children with lots of experience writing these must-know words, too.

So what are you waiting for? Put Fun Flaps into the hands of your students, and watch their literacy skills soar!

Happy Learning,

Violet Findley

P.S. Once kids have mastered the first 100 sight words, be sure to introduce them to the second 100 sight words via *Fun Flaps: 2nd 100 Sight Words*!

MAKING FUN FLAPS

Making Fun Flaps is so easy. Just reproduce a copy for each child then follow these simple directions.

(1) Cut out the Fun Flap along the dashed lines, so you have a square shape.

(2) OPTIONAL: Invite children to color the square shape—and pictures—to make the Fun Flap extra engaging.

(3) Place the Fun Flap on a flat surface with the blank side facing up.

(4) Fold back the four corners along the solid lines so they touch in the center of the square.

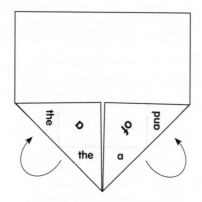

(5) Turn over the Fun Flap. Fold back the corners again so that they touch the center of the square.

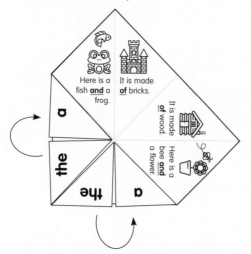

(6) Fold the Fun Flap in half.

(7) Place your right thumb and index finger inside the two right flaps.

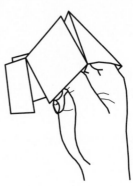

(8) Place your left thumb and index finger inside the two left flaps.

(9) Open and close the Fun Flap by moving your fingers.

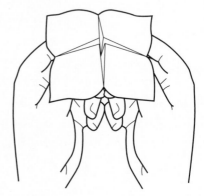

(10) Have fun!

TIP

We've included a blank template (and companion writing page), so you—and your students—can create original Fun Flaps to practice additional sight words.

USING FUN FLAPS

Using Fun Flaps is so entertaining. Just follow these simple directions.

1. Partner A holds the fun flap in a closed position, so that the points touch. Partner A asks partner B to choose one of the four featured sight words and a number from 1–10.

2. Partner B chooses a sight word (*the*) and a number (6).

3. Partner A opens and closes the fun flap that many times, inviting Partner B to find the same sight word on the four interior flaps.

4. Partner B points to the sight word (*the*) and reads it aloud.

5. Partner A lifts the flap to reveal a corresponding picture and sight-word sentence (Look at *the* dog.), inviting partner B to read it.

6. Partner B reads the sight-word sentence aloud. Tip: Partner A can provide help if necessary.

7. Partners A and B switch roles.

8. Reinforce sight-word learning by encouraging children to use the companion pages to practice writing the featured sight words.

FIVE GREAT WAYS
TO USE THE FUN FLAPS

1 Assign partners five minutes of "Fun Flap playtime" at the beginning and/or end of each school day.

2 Place Fun Flaps in a center for kids to enjoy at designated times.

3 Invite classroom volunteers to share Fun Flaps with struggling readers.

4 Send Fun Flaps home so kids can practice their sight words with caregivers.

5 Host a "Fun Flap party," in which kids circulate around the room and use the manipulatives with several different classmates.

TIP

Use Fun Flaps as a way to get students acquainted with one another. Draw names from a hat to pick random partners and foster new friendships!

For a quick and easy assessment technique, type or write the 100 sight words from the fun flaps on separate cards. Next copy the Sight Word Assessment sheets on pages 62 and 63. These sheets allow for individual assessment. Shuffle the sight word cards and hold them up at random for the child to read. If the child reads the word correctly make a ✔ on the sheet. If the child reads the card incorrectly, make an **X**. Then use the fun flaps to reteach the words as needed.

SIGHT WORD ASSESSMENT   PART 1

Student's Name: _____

SIGHT WORD	DATE/ ✔ or X	DATE/ ✔ or X	SIGHT WORD	DATE/ ✔ or X	DATE/ ✔ or X
the			or		
of			one		
and			had		
a			by		
to			word		
in			but		
is			not		
you			what		
that			all		
it			were		
he			we		
was			when		
for			your		
on			can		
are			said		
as			there		
with			use		
his			an		
they			each		
I			which		
at			she		
be			do		
this			how		
have			their		
from			if		

62

SIGHT WORD ASSESSMENT   PART 2

Student's Name: _____

SIGHT WORD	DATE/ ✔ or X	DATE/ ✔ or X	SIGHT WORD	DATE/ ✔ or X	DATE/ ✔ or X
will			number		
up			no		
other			way		
about			could		
out			people		
many			my		
then			than		
them			first		
these			water		
so			been		
some			called		
her			who		
would			am		
make			its		
like			now		
him			find		
into			long		
time			down		
has			day		
look			did		
two			get		
more			come		
write			made		
go			may		
see			part		

63

Connection to the Standards

Using Fun Flaps supports the standards for Reading Foundational Skills for students in grades K–2.

Foundational Skills
Read common high-frequency words by sight.

Print Concepts
Demonstrate understanding of the organization of the basic features of print.

Phonological Awareness
Demonstrate understanding of spoken words, syllables, and sounds.

Fluency
Read with sufficient accuracy and fluency to support comprehension.

Speaking and Listening
Participate in collaborative conversations about age-appropriate topics.

Source: Copyright © 2010 National Governors Association Center for Best Practices and Council of Chief State Officers. All rights reserved.

© Scholastic Inc.

100 SIGHT WORDS

(From the Fry List)

the	at	there	some	my
of	be	use	her	than
and	this	an	would	first
a	have	each	make	water
to	from	which	like	been
in	or	she	him	called
is	one	do	into	who
you	had	how	time	am
that	by	their	has	its
it	word	if	look	now
he	but	will	two	find
was	not	up	more	long
for	what	other	write	down
on	all	about	go	day
are	were	out	see	did
as	we	many	number	get
with	when	then	no	come
his	your	them	way	made
they	can	these	could	may
I	said	so	people	part

FEATURED SIGHT WORDS

the   of   and   a

Cut and fold the fun flap.

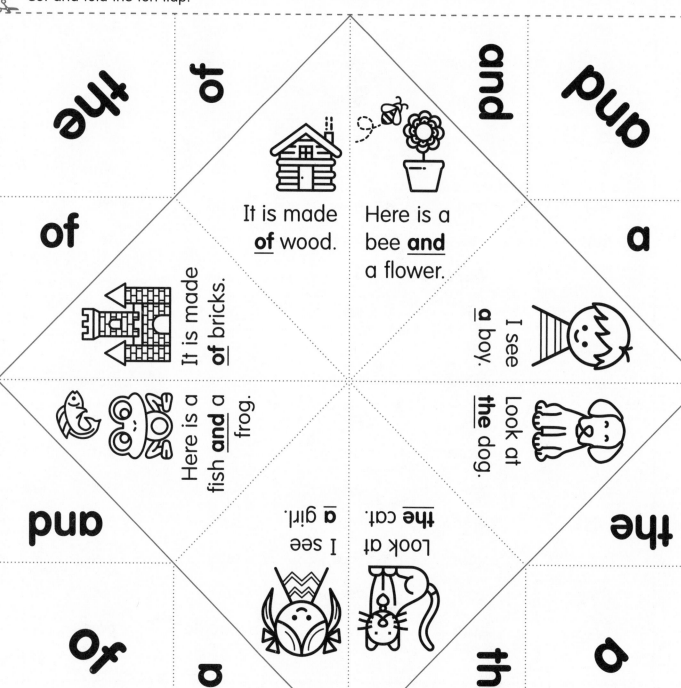

the

of

and

and

of

a

It is made **of** wood.

Here is a bee **and** a flower.

It is made **of** bricks.

I see **a** boy.

Here is a fish **and** a frog.

Look at **the** dog.

and

the

I see **a** girl.

Look at **the** cat.

of

a

the

a

Name: _____

Trace then write each word.

the the the the the the

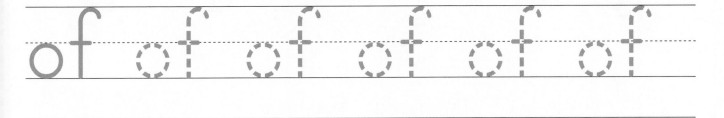

and and and and

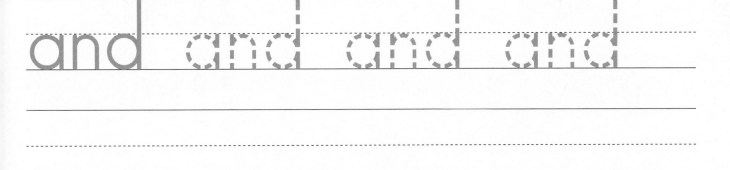

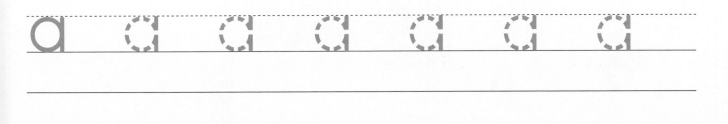

FEATURED SIGHT WORDS

to   in   is   you

Cut and fold the fun flap.

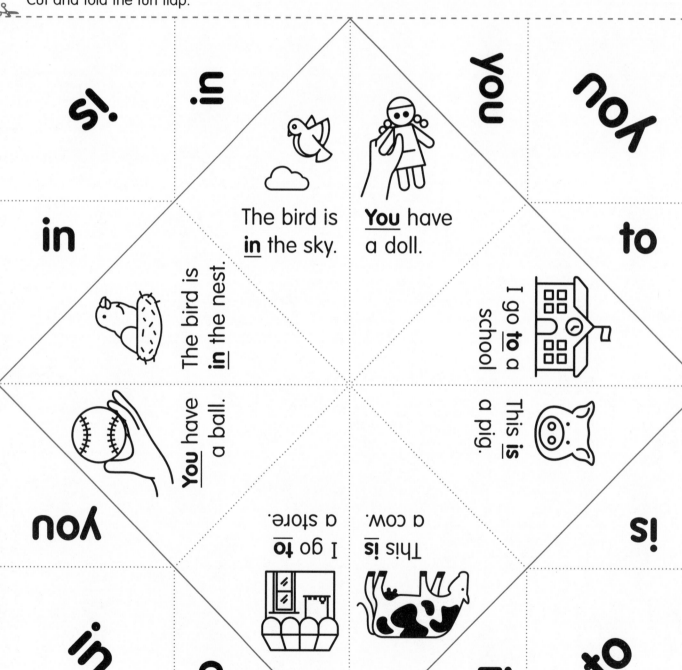

is

in

you

you

in

to

The bird is **in** the sky.

You have a doll.

The bird is **in** the nest.

I go **to** a school

This **is** a pig.

You have a ball.

you

is

I go **to** a store.

This **is** a cow.

in

to

is

to

Name: _____

Trace then write each word.

to to to to to to

in in in in in in in

is is is is is is is is

you you you you

FEATURED SIGHT WORDS

that   it   he   was

Cut and fold the fun flap.

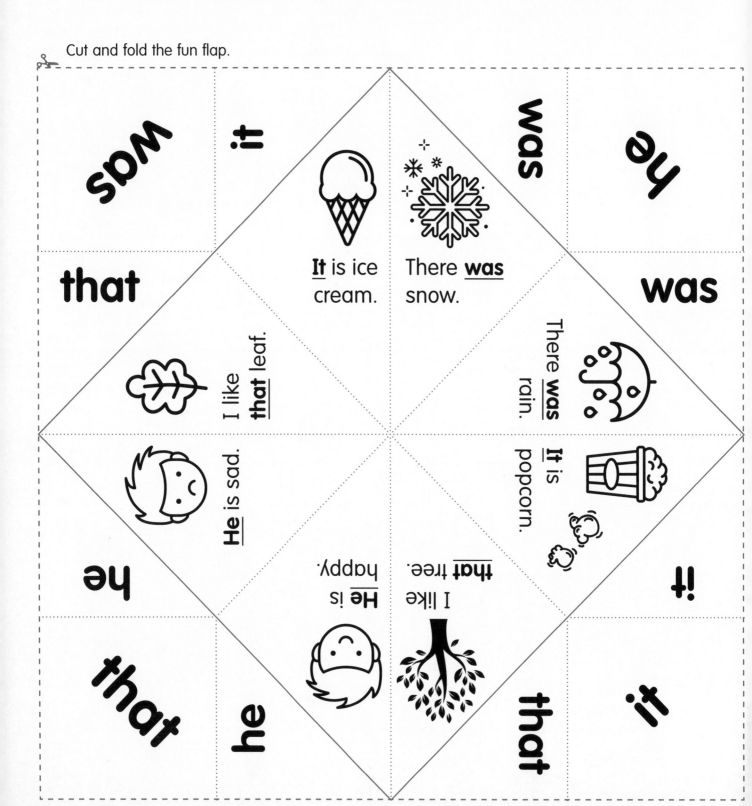

Name: _____

Trace then write each word.

that that that that

it it it it it it it it

he he he he he he

was was was was

FEATURED SIGHT WORDS

for   on   are   as

Cut and fold the fun flap.

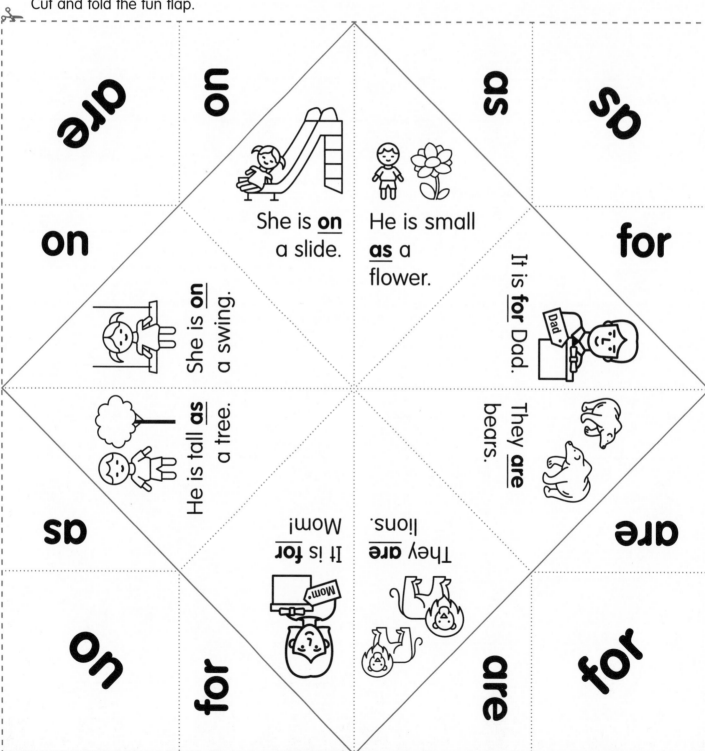

are

on

as

sɒ

on

for

She is **on** a swing.

It is **for** Dad.

He is tall **as** a tree.

They **are** bears.

sɒ

ǝɹɒ

She is **on** a slide.

He is small **as** a flower.

It is **for** Mom!

They **are** lions.

on

for

are

for

Name: _____

Trace then write each word.

for for for for for

on on on on on on

are are are are

as as as as as as

with	she	they	I

Cut and fold the fun flap.

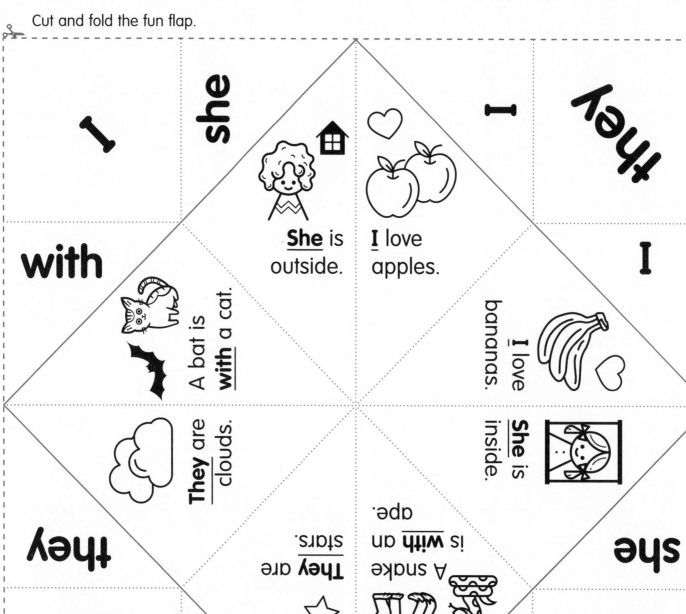

She is outside.

I love apples.

A bat is **with** a cat.

I love bananas.

She is inside.

They are clouds.

A snake is **with** an ape.

They are stars.

Name: _____

Trace then write each word.

with with with with

she she she she

they they they they

I I I I I I I

FEATURED SIGHT WORDS

at   be   this   have

Cut and fold the fun flap.

this

be

be

have

She will **be** happy.

I **have** short hair.

be

at

have

have

at

He is **at** home.

This is a pig.

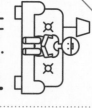

this

She will **be** sad.

I **have** long hair.

He is **at** school.

This is a horse.

be

at

this

at

Name: _____

Trace then write each word.

at at at at at at

be be be be be

this this this this

have have have

FEATURED SIGHT WORDS

from   or   one   had

Cut and fold the fun flap.

one

or

or

had

had

from

one

from

or

Should I read **or** write?

He **had** candy.

Should I swing **or** slide?

I am **from** Earth.

He **had** flowers.

Here is **one** fish.

I am **from** Mars.

Here is **one** crab.

one

from

Name: _____

Trace then write each word.

from from from from

or or or or or or

one one one one

had had had had

FEATURED SIGHT WORDS

by   word   but   not

Cut and fold the fun flap.

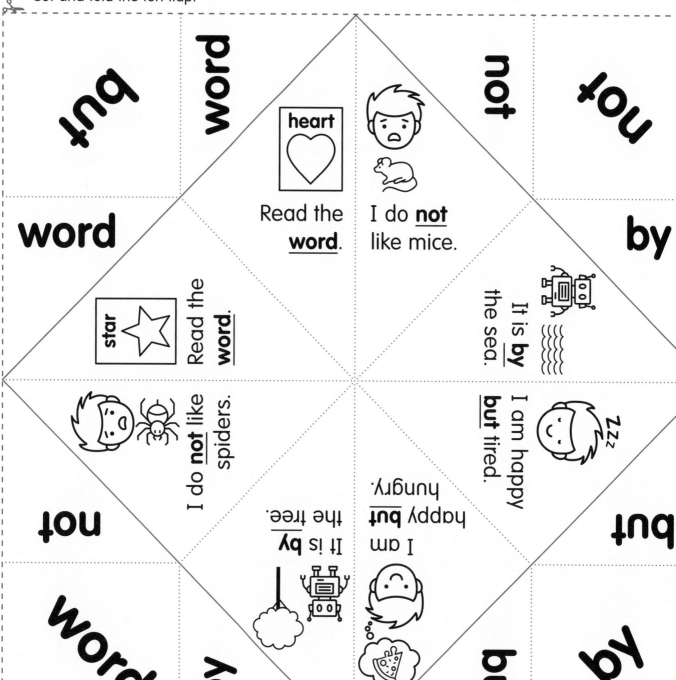

Name: _____

Trace then write each word.

by by by by by by

word word word

but but but but but

not not not not not

FEATURED SIGHT WORDS

what   all   were   we

Cut and fold the fun flap.

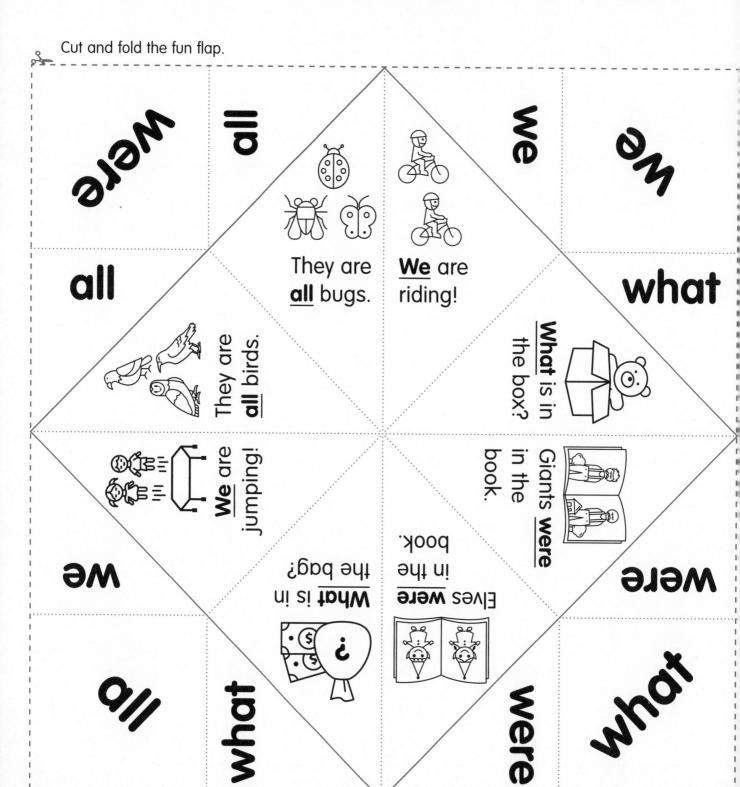

Name: _____

Trace then write each word.

what what what

all all all all all all

were were were

we we we we we

FEATURED SIGHT WORDS

when your can said

Cut and fold the fun flap.

can

your

said

said

your

when

Here is **your** money.

She **said** goodbye!

Goodbye!

Here is **your** key.

I like **when** it is sunny.

He **said** hello!

Hello!

A plane **can** fly.

said

I like **when** it is snowy.

A kite **can** fly.

can

your

when

can

when

Name: _____

Trace then write each word.

when when when

your your your

can can can can

said said said said

FEATURED SIGHT WORDS

there   use   an   each

Cut and fold the fun flap.

an

use

use

each

use

each

there

an

there

I **use** a pencil.

Each girl has a crown.

I **use** a crayon.

Each boy has a hat.

There is a rabbit.

An elephant is big.

There is a turtle.

An ant is small.

Name: _____

Trace then write each word.

there there there

use use use use

an an an an an an

each each each

FEATURED SIGHT WORDS

which   his   do   how

Cut and fold the fun flap.

do

his

how

how

his

which

His frog is silly.

How will it get down?

His frog is silly.

How will it get down?

Which pig is sleeping?

His dog is silly.

I **do** like pizza!

How will it get up?

how

which

I **do** like popcorn!

Which owl is sleeping?

his

which

do

do

which

op

Name: _____

Trace then write each word.

which which which

his his his his his

do do do do do

how how how how

FEATURED SIGHT WORDS

their   if   will   up

✂ Cut and fold the fun flap.

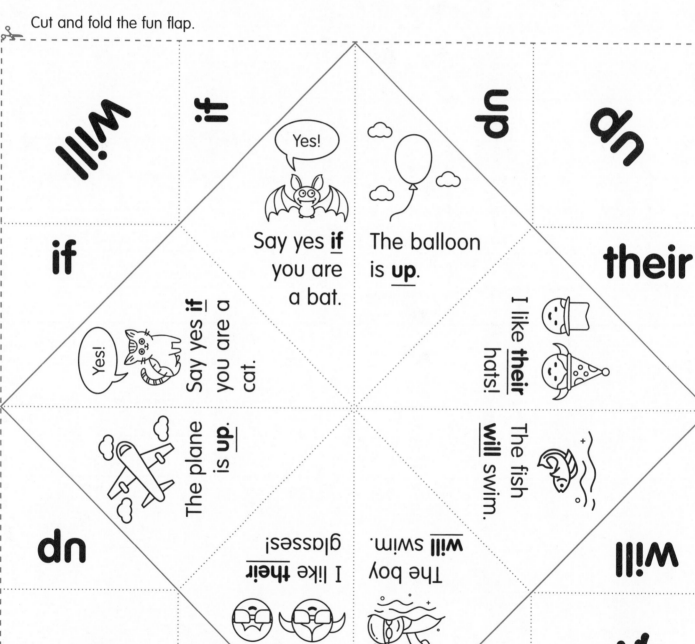

Name: _____

Trace then write each word.

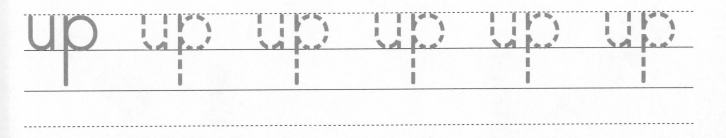

FEATURED SIGHT WORDS

other about out many

Cut and fold the fun flap.

out

about

many

many

about

other

This book is **about** lions.

I see **many** gumballs.

This book is **about** bears.

I want the **other** cupcake.

I see **many** butterflies.

The fish jumped **out**!

I want the **other** cookie.

The frog jumped **out**!

many

out

about

other

out

other

Name: _____

Trace then write each word.

other other other

about about about

out out out out

many many many

FEATURED SIGHT WORDS

then them these so

Cut and fold the fun flap.

so

then

then

so

then

them

I ran **then** I swam.

He is **so** scary!

I ran **then** I rode.

He is **so** hairy!

I see **them**.

These smell good.

These smell bad.

I wear **them**.

so

them

these

them

so

these

them

these

Name: _____

Trace then write each word.

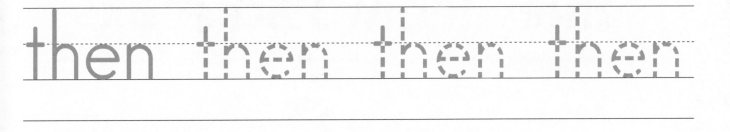

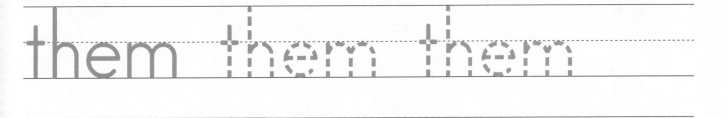

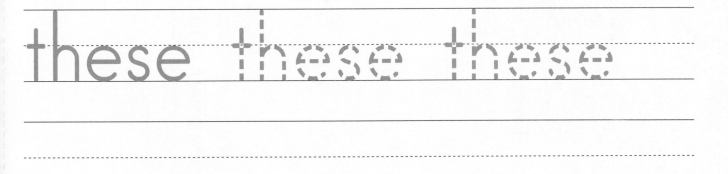

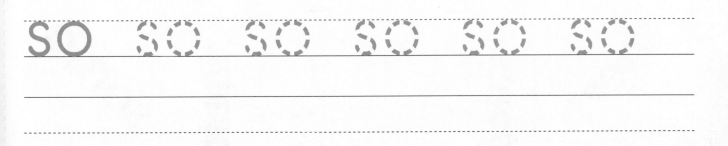

FUN FLAP 16
FEATURED SIGHT WORDS
some her would make

Cut and fold the fun flap.

would

her

make

make

her

some

I like **her** skirt.

I **make** a cake.

I like **her** pants.

Here are **some** triangles.

I **make** cookies.

Would you like soup?

Here are **some** squares.

Would you like pie?

make

some

her

would

some

Name: _____

Trace then write each word.

some some some

her her her her

would would would

make make make

FEATURED SIGHT WORDS

like him into time

Cut and fold the fun flap.

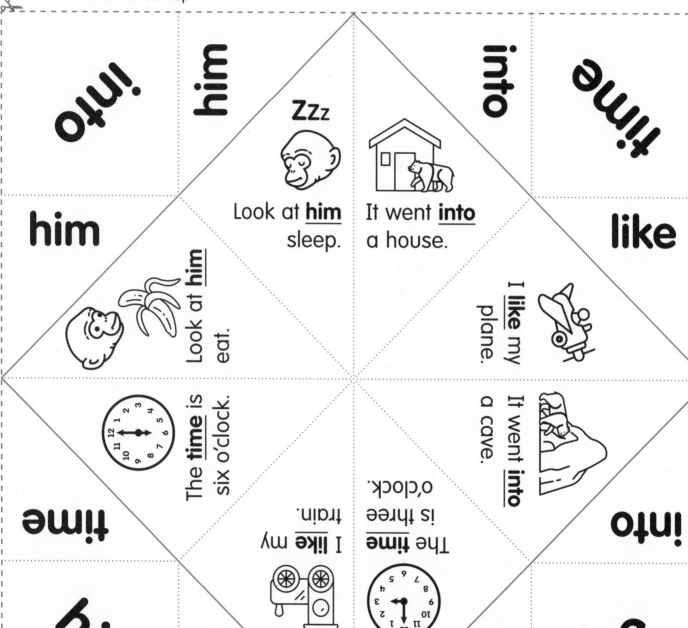

Name: _____

Trace then write each word.

like like like like like

him him him him

into into into into

time time time time

FEATURED SIGHT WORDS

has   look   two   more

Cut and fold the fun flap.

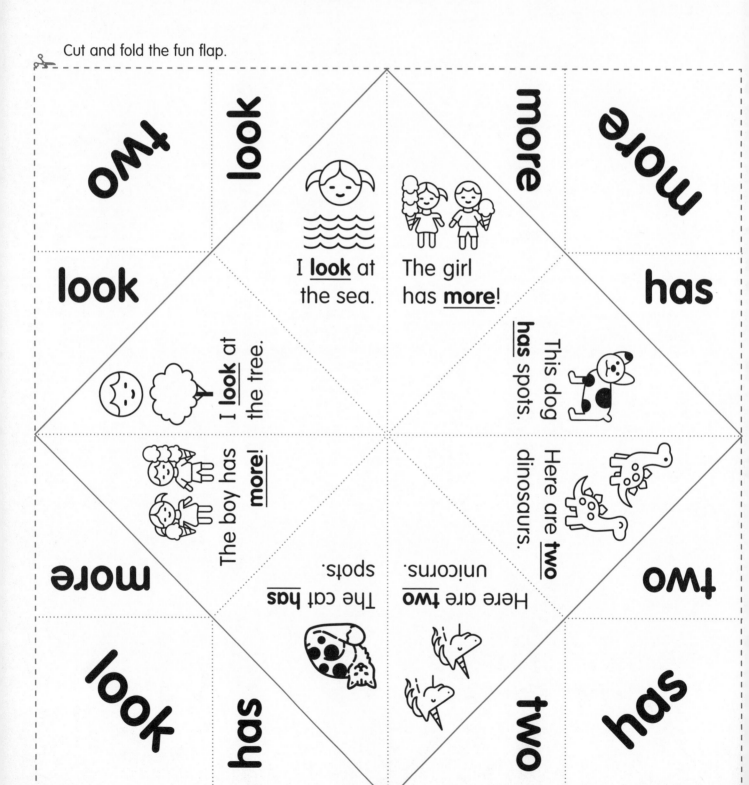

Name: _____

Trace then write each word.

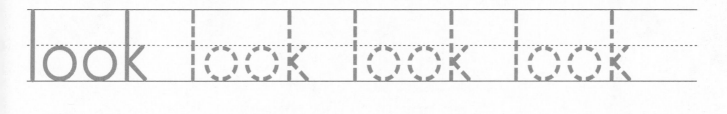

FEATURED SIGHT WORDS

write go see number

Cut and fold the fun flap.

see

go

number

number

go

write

I **go** home.

This magic **number** is 10.

10

I **write** my name.

Ann

I **go** to school.

I **see** a duck.

This magic **number** is 7.

7

I **write** my name.

Jim

I **see** a truck.

see

number

go

write

see

write

Name: _____

Trace then write each word.

write write write

go go go go go

see see see see

number number

FEATURED SIGHT WORDS

no way could people

Cut and fold the fun flap.

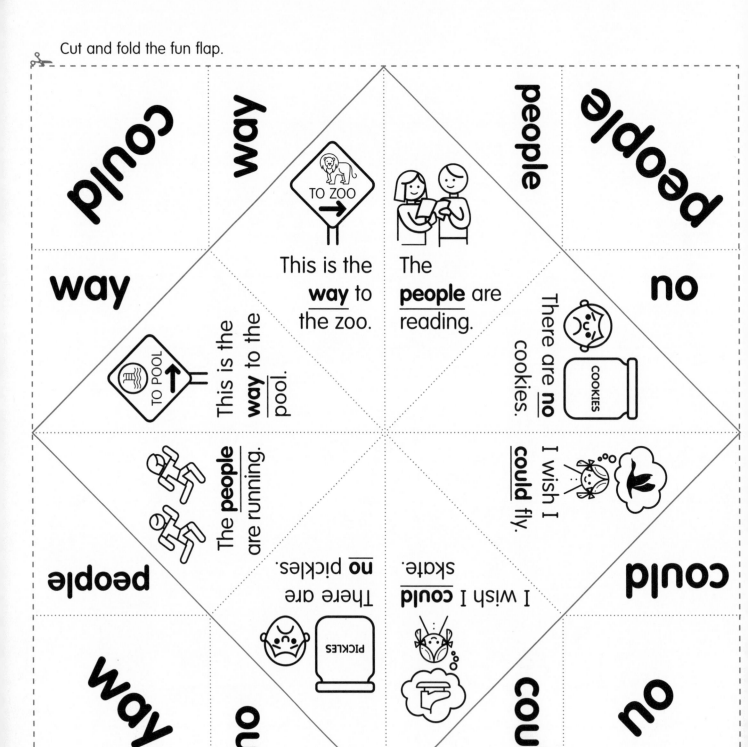

Name: _____

Trace then write each word.

no no no no no no

way way way way

could could could

people people

FEATURED SIGHT WORDS

my than first water

Cut and fold the fun flap.

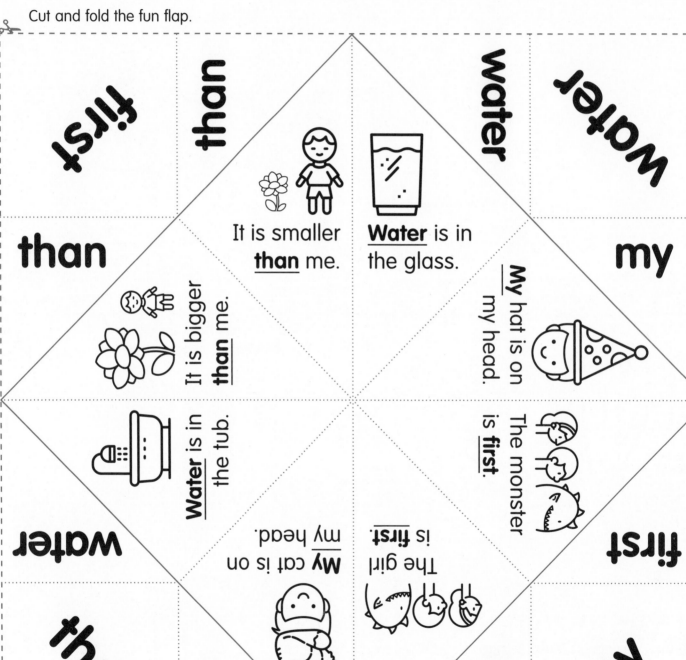

first

than

water

water

than

my

It is smaller **than** me.

Water is in the glass.

It is bigger **than** me.

My hat is on my head.

Water is in the tub.

The monster is **first**.

water

My cat is on my head.

The girl is **first**.

first

than

my

first

my

Name: _____

Trace then write each word.

my my my my my

than than than than

first first first first

water water water

FEATURED SIGHT WORDS

been called who am

Cut and fold the fun flap.

who

called

am

am

called

been

He is **called** Ben.

I **am** a doctor.

She is **called** Jen.

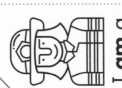

He has **been** eating.

I **am** a firefighter.

Who is on the bike?

He has **been** sleeping.

Who is in the car?

am

who

called

been

who

been

Name: _____

Trace then write each word.

been been been

called called called

who who who who

am am am am am

FEATURED SIGHT WORDS

its   now   find   long

Cut and fold the fun flap.

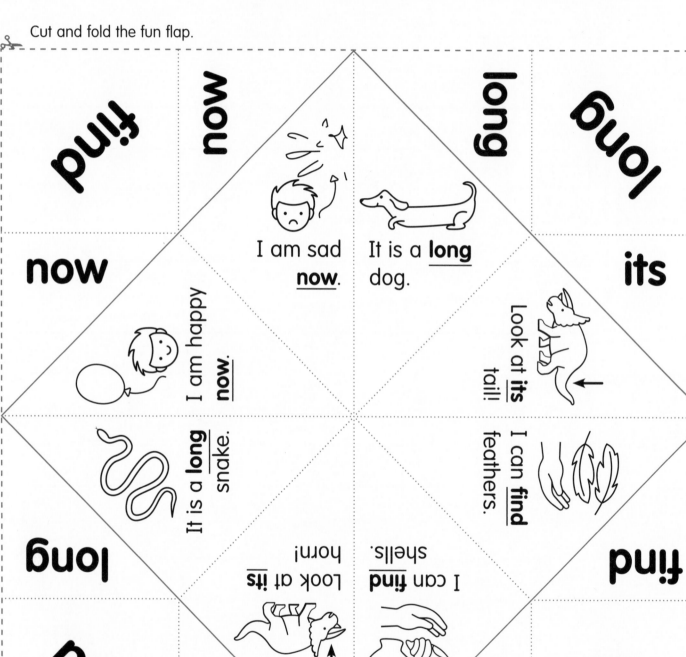

- I am sad **now**.
- It is a **long** dog.
- I am happy **now**.
- Look at **its** tail!
- I can **find** feathers.
- It is a **long** snake.
- Look at **its** horn!
- I can **find** shells.

find   now   long   long

now   its

long   find

now   its   find   its

Name: _____

Trace then write each word.

its its its its its its

now now now now

find find find find

long long long long

FEATURED SIGHT WORDS

down   day   did   get

Cut and fold the fun flap.

did

day

get

get

day

down

It is NOT **day**.

I **get** two lollipops.

It is **day**.

He goes **down**.

I **get** one lollipop.

The rabbit **did** hop.

She goes **down**.

The rabbit **did** eat.

get

down

did

day

down

did

down

Name: _____

Trace then write each word.

down down down

day day day day

did did did did

get get get get

FEATURED SIGHT WORDS

come made may part

Cut and fold the fun flap.

may

made

part

part

made

come

It is **made** of snow.

I see **part** of a deer.

Come to the beach!

It is **made** of candy.

You **may** have a banana.

I see **part** of a rabbit.

Come to the mountain!

You **may** have an apple.

part

come

may

made

come

may

come

Name: _____

Trace then write each word.

come come come

made made made

may may may may

part part part part

FEATURED SIGHT WORDS

Cut and fold the fun flap.

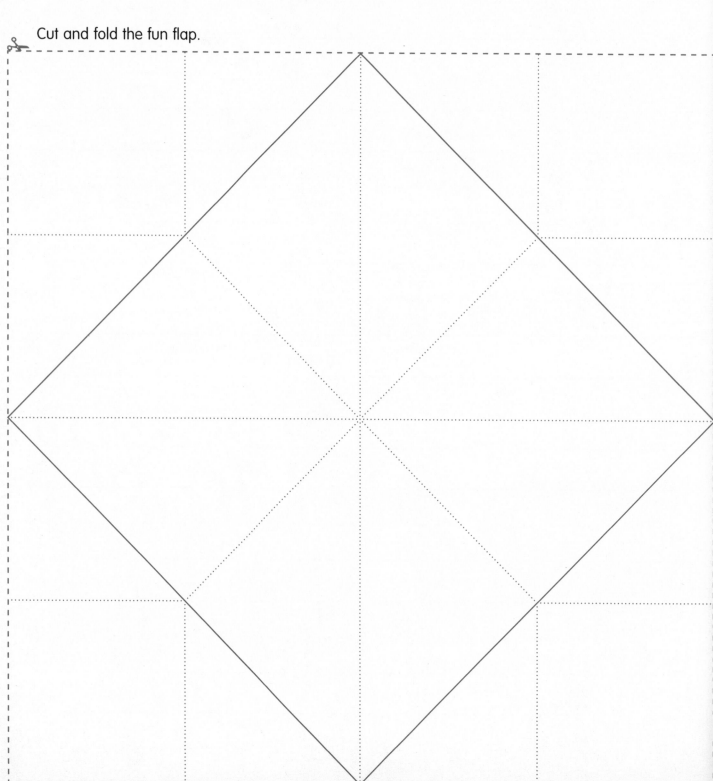

Name: _____

SIGHT WORD ASSESSMENT PART 1

Student's Name: _____

SIGHT WORD	DATE/ ✔ or X	DATE/ ✔ or X	SIGHT WORD	DATE/ ✔ or X	DATE/ ✔ or X
the			or		
of			one		
and			had		
a			by		
to			word		
in			but		
is			not		
you			what		
that			all		
it			were		
he			we		
was			when		
for			your		
on			can		
are			said		
as			there		
with			use		
his			an		
they			each		
I			which		
at			she		
be			do		
this			how		
have			their		
from			if		

62

Student's Name: _____

SIGHT WORD	DATE/ ✔ or X	DATE/ ✔ or X	SIGHT WORD	DATE/ ✔ or X	DATE/ ✔ or X
will			number		
up			no		
other			way		
about			could		
out			people		
many			my		
then			than		
them			first		
these			water		
so			been		
some			called		
her			who		
would			am		
make			its		
like			now		
him			find		
into			long		
time			down		
has			day		
look			did		
two			get		
more			come		
write			made		
go			may		
see			part		

NOTES